My Ball Turret Bombing Missions Over Europe

(And a Few Screw-Ups)

As Told In Henry G. Smith's Diary
and Personal Contact

Compiled and Written by
B.J. Bryan
Co- Author Henry G. Smith

HIGHLANDS PUBLISHING

Copyrights and Credits:

Title- My Ball Turret Bombing Missions Over Europe and a Few Screw Ups

Author–B.J. Bryan

Co- Author Henry G. Smith

My Ball Turret Bombing Missions Over Europe and a Few Screw Ups Text copyright © 2015

ISBN(13) 978-1584780601

BISAC: BIO008000
BIOGRAPHY & AUTOBIOGRAPHY / Military

Printed in the United States of America
First Edition /First Printing 2016

DEDICATION

DEDICATED TO:

PUGET SOUND HONOR GUARD
AND
HONOR GUARD NETWORK

TABLE OF CONTENTS

Foreward

ARMY AIR CORPS WORLD WAR II BALL TURRET
GUNNER AND A MEMBER OF THE GREATEST
GENERATION

8TH ARMY AIR CORPS, 92ND BOMBER GROUP
BASED AT PODINGTON, ENGLAND

29 APRIL TO 17 SEPTEMBER, 1944

On 23 November 2013, I received a large envelope from
my oldest son who is an Air Force Reservist, and takes his
weekend "warrior duty" at Fort McCloud, Washington.
(Fort Lewis (Army base) and Fort McChord (Air Force
base) have been combined and is now known as Joint Base
Lewis-McChord.) He had been talking several months about
something that an airman he knew would be sending him
that should be sent to me. This was it!

There was a letter enclosed written by Barbara Schwartz to a David Timney explaining she had these papers of Henry G. Smith who wished his diary to be published but kept them on her desk for years as she never knew an author. She is with the Puget Sound Honor Flight, which flies World War II veterans to Washington, D.C., in order to see the memorials there for the many wars the country has participated in over the years but especially the World War II memorial.

I had the opportunity to see the memorial several years ago and it was a magnificent sight to see and behold. The faces of the statues from the Korean Conflict are astonishing and as long as I live, I will never forget the expressions. I also saw the statute of the Iwo Jima servicemen raising of the American flag. Seeing all the statutes was heart warming. I'll go into that further later on as to how I got to Washington, D.C.

9 January 2014 – Email from Duane Wolfe, President of the 92nd Bomber Group Memorial Association saying he had information on Henry G. Smith. The group name was "Fame's Favored Few" and was assigned to the 40th Combat Wing; this was the oldest group in the 8th Air Force having been the first USAAF bomber group to make the transatlantic crossing to the United Kingdom in July 1942.

He asked for my phone number which I sent him.

10 January 2014 – Telephone call from Duane Wolfe. "Hank" attended the picnic last year with his wife. He was awarded the cover they wear in their group and was pleased to receive it. Mr. Wolfe said he would send my email to Hank

as he had tried calling last night and again this morning, but the phone was busy.

Mr. Hutchins, who was the Historian for the UK Podington Group, has passed. I am now to contact Greg Alexander for additional information.

This story is taken from Mr. Smith's own manually type-written notes. All I have done is to make spelling corrections. Some of the names have been changed as was his wish during our telephone conversation on 13 January 2014, as he didn't want to create any problems for others or himself. He approved my inserting other names in their places and did so. On 29 January 2014, I received his permission to do the above and as I reiterated to him, I would send a rough draft for his approval when I have completed the diary. I also received photographs of him in uniform, one of him at 89 years of age, as well as others. It is very interesting to say the least.

In order to get information about his outfit and base he flew from I got from the Internet until I get responses to my letters I wrote to the two people whom I don't know.

I had a telephone call from a World War II veteran and friend of Hank's who has the name of a place and the address in order for me to get additional information. The person, Duane Wolfe, is the president of the 92nd Bomber Group UAAAF-USAF Memorial Association and said he not only knew "Hank" but that Hank and his wife had attended Mr. Wolfe's outfit's picnic last year and was awarded their cap as an honor for being present at the meeting. Mr. Wolfe forwarded to the Smiths my email and I received one from Fay Smith that same evening. (See additional dates above of 9 January and 10 January 2014.)

What is a ball turret gunner, you ask? Well, that is the gunner who sits in a dome or structure for guns as on a warship, tank, or airplane. In this case, it is a B-17 airplane. I'm sure you've seen them in war movies and it is generally small in stature and height. I don't know about you but I'd be scared out of my wits as he has no protection from enemy fire unless his comrades were firing at the enemy as well.

•In my conversation with Hank and Fay Smith I told him I wanted information about him as people who read this book will want information about him as well and not just what he did so here goes!

Chapter 1
My Story

I was born in Seattle, Washington, 28 December 1922, and was reared in a community called Rainier Beach located in the south end of Seattle. My middle name is George. I was drafted into the Army at Fort Lewis, Washington and assigned to the Air Corps and sent off to Fresno, California for basic training.

Stretching my memory capabilities, I went to Lowry, Colorado for gunnery training. After training I was assigned to a B-17 crew as a ball turret gunner and we flew to Ireland. (I got the job of ball turret gunner because no one else wanted the job, so I volunteered – the most dangerous on the plane). From Ireland we took a train to a base in England called Podington.

During the time the Nazis were trying to destroy Great Britain, Winston S. Churchill, Prime Minister, was ordering more bases to be built between 1940 and 1942 to accommodate two Royal Air Force squadrons in order to offer more protection from the enemy. This was one of those bases built but drag-racing enthusiasts wanted to use the main runway as a drag-racing strip and in 1964 it became the Santa Pod Raceway opening during the Easter weekend, 1966. Some buildings remain though most have succumbed to vandalism or demolition. The two main hangers are gone – one dismantled, the other lost in a fire. The old control tower is one of the few to have been converted into an unusual private home.

When I started my tour the required number of missions to complete was 25. As the Allies gained control of the air space in France and Germany our bombing missions were increased to 30, then 35. I flew all 35 of those.

Then the Air Force installed extra radio equipment in a B-17 and I flew an additional 17 missions.

I was sent back to the States to Walla Walla, Washington, where I worked in the Personnel Affairs Office because I could type. After my discharge I tried 22 different trades before settling down in the printing business. My apprenticeship was at the Seattle Post Intelligencer, and then moved to Tacoma where I worked as a Journeyman for the Tacoma News Tribune. In 1961 I purchased a printing business in Puyallup, Washington before retiring in 1988.

Back to how I (the author) got to see the memorials in Washington, D.C., at age 71, I rode on the back seat of a motorcycle all across the country – over 4,000 miles! It was a real adventure seeing the beautiful country, people saluting the United States flags the motorcyclists carried, etc. It is called Run for the Wall and now. There is the Central Route and the Southern Route. We went the Central Route (the middle states) but I could fill a book just about what happened along the way. I'm trying o find a way across again but looking for someone who has a side car as I just recently turned 80! The Run for the Wall was begun by 3 Vietnam veterans who didn't get a welcome home.

Well, they do now.

Chapter 2
My 35 Day Missions
Over Europe

BERLIN, GERMANY
4 May 1944

Well, today we got in our first mission. We made the formation and crossed the channel. We got about 40 minutes from the target and the mission was cancelled. We saw some flak just as we crossed the coast but it was way behind us and low. It looked kind of funny – just some black puffs in the sky but I guess it won't look so funny when we get close enough to get a real good look. We didn't see any more flak coming back. I guess the weather was pretty bad over the target to make us turn back after going so far. Well, we got credit for the mission so it's O.K. by me.

Bomb load – 3 – 1.000 lb. Demolition

30 – 100 lb. Incendiaries

Incendiary weapons are weapons to start fires or destroy sensitive equipment. They are not explosives per se but are designed to ignite rather than detonate.

BERLIN, GERMANY
7 May 1944

We could not find the formation today. We went from group-to-group watching the colors of the flares but could not find anybody shooting our color. So after we looked over four or five groups we just tagged onto the next one that came along. I'm not sure whose fault it was: Neimys or Hannigan's.

Over the channel I noticed frozen oil coming from the inspection plate so I told Neimy that oil was coming from #1 engine so we aborted and feathered it.

We dropped our bombs in the channel. We flew with our own crew today. We had a different co-pilot with us the first time. He had in 16 missions.

Bomb load – 3 – 1,000 lb. Demolition
5 – 500 lb Incendiaries

MERSEBURG, GERMANY
12 May 1944

We were hit by flak as we crossed the channel today and hit some more of it at the target which was a synthetic oil plant. I noticed four fires going that the group ahead of us had started as we were coming in. I saw one large fire that we started. I was following our own bombs down but we hit some slip-stream and I lost our bombs in the clouds. I wasn't paying much attention to the flak as I was busy watching the bombs. I guess there was quite a bit of it though because we got some holes in the plane. We bombed the target at 27,000 feet.

Bomb load – 16—300 lb. G.P. Demolition

STETTIN POLAND (NOW SZCZECIN)
13 May 1944

We missed the primary that was Poznan, Poland. Stettin was in German hands until 1945, and so we decided to hit our secondary targets so we swung around and hit Stettin. I saw another group over it before we swung around to make a pass at it. It was smoking then. I didn't see any fires going and I didn't see any bombs hit because it was pretty cloudy. It was a hell of a long trip today, 1,860 miles! We flew over the North Sea to Denmark, crossed the Baltic Sea, missed Kiel and went into Poland. Then we swung back. Our primary target was Poznan, Poland. That is a Focke-Wulf plant (built German planes) and we missed our proper formation again.

The group behind us got hit by fighters today. I saw two B-17s go down from the group behind. I saw seven parachutes from the first plane and one from the other plane. The second B-17 blew up when it hit the ground. A Focke-Wulf 190 (FW) was unquestionably the most valuable German fighter aircraft of the war. It was conceived as the successor to the Messrschmitt as early as 1937, and a pro-type flew in June 1939. The FM blew up in mid-air.

We got heavy flak over the target and flak from four or five other places along the way. A B-17 ditched about five miles from the English coast. It sure must be tough going down so close to home. We could hear him over the V.H.F. (very high frequency) giving his position. We flew back over the channel at about 500 feet. We had bombed the target at 23,000 feet.

Bomb load – 10 – 500 lb. Demolition

BERLIN, GERMANY
19 May 1944

We hit the target at 26,000 feet. The flak was moderate but they almost had our number. I saw the bombs hit but it was pretty cloudy so I didn't get to see very much of Berlin. No large fires were going that I could see.

Flak burst between our ship and ship 071. I heard it hit our ship and it shot out the control cables from #1 engine and #4 was smoking. We feathered #1 but stayed in formation until we hit the North Sea. Then we couldn't keep up with them as the other engines had been hit and we couldn't get enough out of them so they left us as we let down.

Neimy said we might not be able to make it back so we threw out all the ammunition and I took the sight out of the turret and prepared to drop it to maintain altitude. It is funny but I was sure we'd make it O.K. but everybody else had their doubts.

A piece of flak just missed Grayson. He was throwing chaff (anything worthless) out the hatch and he just leaned back to pick up another bundle and a piece came up just missing his foot and went out through the edge of the hatch.

We made it to base before the rest of the formation. All engines were damaged. The ground crew did not see how we made it back. So, I guess we were lucky as hell at that because those boys know what they're talking about. The Crew Chief counted over 100 flak holes in the ship. We had a Bombardier Navigator. The fighter escorts consisting of P-38s and P-51s were wonderful

Bomb load – 42 –100 lb. Incendiaries

20 May 1944

Three planes blew up on formation today. I was in bed when it happened. It was foggy out. The first ship started to take off and could not make it so he turned around and started back. The second ship had already started and it hit the first one head on. One of them exploded and the concussion set off another ship at the end of the runway. The other ship caught fire, and then blew up. Seven or eight men got out. The waist gunner saw what was going to happen so he got out and started running.

We walked out by the wreckage and found a body or rather half a body from the waist up about 300 yards from the ship. He must have been blown along the ground because there was a path of blood all the way from the ship. The body was burned black but he had all his teeth. We could see them from what was left of his face. Funny they were not all blown out.

Another ship ran off the runway landing and banged up all his props. I don't think that we will fly for a few days until they get the runways fixed. Ship 090 is in the sub-depot getting repairs anyway.

SAARBRUCKEN, GERMANY
23 May 1944

There was very thick cloud coverage. We could not see bombs at all after they went through the clouds. Chaff (metal strips thrown out of the plane to confuse the German ground radar and Radar equipment worked beautifully). Moderate flak was way off between us and the next group. We bombed the target at approximately 23,000 feet. Grayson was throwing out chaff when a piece of flak just missed him.

This morning we had an alert as we were going to the planes. We sat in the trucks for about a half hour; then we started out to the ship with the lights on parking. We stopped at one ship and as the driver was backing up, he bumped into a gas truck. Somebody said it was gas and we all jumped out of the truck and started running. Jeff got knocked off the truck in the rush and hurt his leg. Talk about a bunch of nervous wrecks! I think I ran about a hundred yards before I slowed down enough to glance back and see if anything was going to explode.

We had a good ship today, had a new tail with the flexible turret. We didn't hit any fighters and had damn good escorts. This was about a 7-hour mission. We were mostly on oxygen. There was heavy fog on take off.

Bomb load – 4 – 1,000 lb Demolition

COTTBUS, GERMANY
29 May 1944

The target was the FW assembly plant in Germany. We started climbing when we left the English coast. We flew a couple of hours at 21,000 feet, then let down to 13,000 feet. We hit a moderate amount of flak around Hamburg and other spots. None hit the target. We hit the target at 13,000 and it was a good thing that there wasn't any flak. Flying at that altitude, they could have thrown rocks at us. The target must have been demolished completely when we left it. I saw bomb bursts all over the entire target and I never even saw one bomb miss the target area.

About 15 minutes from the target we were attacked by about 12 Focke-Wulf 190s. The Focke-Wulf (FW) 190 was unquestionably the most valuable German aircraft fighter of the war. It was conceived as the successor to the Messerschmitt as early as 1937, and a prototype flew in June 1939. Reports said we got nine of them. We lost two planes from our group. McNamara, waist gunner and radio man, got hit. Dave Harris, the waist gunner (McNamara and Harris were both waist gunners, one was on the left, the other the right), got a piece of shell through his arm and I guess it won't ever be the same. It will screw up his ball playing.

We got 20-mms in our right wing behind the gas tank. Lucky as hell it wasn't a few inches further up. I saw two planes and two FWs explode on the ground. There were about 12 parachutes floating around.

A FW 190 was making a pass at the element at (element is the group of B-17s that were above the head plane; there are 12 planes and at times called groups) 9 o'clock and he caught on fire going down. I never saw anybody shooting at him but I could see smoke coming from Fergy's gun so I verified it for him. Boy, he is sure an excitable guy. I happened to be in the waist taking a leak (urinating) when these guys started making passes at us. He started jumping around like mad. I unhooked the other waist gun for Grayson to take and then climbed in the ball. I looked up in the waist after the fighters were gone and Grayson was sitting on the rim of my turret smoking a cigarette and Ferguson was running from one window to the other hunting for more fighters. I laughed myself silly even if it wasn't funny. This was the first time Ferguson flew with us and I guess he wasn't used to taking things so easy.

McNamara was the pilot; Anthony's face was still white and there wasn't a bit of color to his eyes when we got back to the barracks and he was telling me about it. Boy, he was still scared! That's one good thing about our crew, nobody gets excited a bit or if they do, they don't show it.

Bomb load – 10 – 500 lb Demolition

BOULOGNE, FRANCE
4 June 1944
We're hitting the coast in a pre-invasion blitz. We got a raw deal today. We flew spare. We got six minutes from the target, and then turned back. The formation came in right behind us. Sure hate missing these milk runs. We were sure praying for somebody to abort. We had half a notion to tag along anyway and go on in.

Bomb load – 12 – 500 lb Demolition

LONGUES, FRANCE
6 June 1944 (D-Day!)
Well, today was the BIG Day! I got up at 12:30 a.m., and then I ate chow. We didn't have a briefing this morning. Grayson said he heard there were 1,900 planes going up today. Niemy called us outside the tent about 3:30 and told us it was the INVASION. I didn't think anybody would know about it until after it was underway. We took off about 5:05 a.m.

It was a beautiful morning above the clouds at 13,000 feet. The sun was shining on all the formations. Planes were all over the sky. It seems kind of funny on such a beautiful day I could appreciate such beauty and know that in a few hours or so I would be participating in mass slaughter. Well, I had no regrets knowing the type of people we were going to kill.

I tried to see the channel and get a look at all the ships I knew must be below but the clouds were about 5,000 feet thick. I saw a few ships and a couple destroyers just before the target. I noticed about five yellow flashes from the destroyers. Our target was a 4-gun installation.

We bombed P.F.F. (Path Finder Formation) at 07.05 a.m. Invasion was due to start at 07.23. We had orders not to drop our bombs after 07.25.

There was so much traffic in the air today that we never turned directly back but went over France for about 45 minutes.

I saw a few of these rockets we've been hearing about and they were very inaccurate. There was no flak at all and no enemy fighters which sure surprised me. I figured they were saving the Luftwaffe (German Air Force) for just this occasion. I expect the boys will hit fighters tonight though.

Coming back I saw a convoy about mid-channel for a few seconds and more on the English coast. I saw lots of gliders parked on bases in England and a bomb dump.

Weather was rough as hell coming in.

Bomb load – 12—500 lb Demolition

LORIENT/HERLIN/BASTARD, GERMANY
7 June 1944

We hit an airfield two miles south or Lorient. The first group hit the left side and we hit the right. Our target was personnel barracks and hangers. We bombed at 23,000 feet. I could not make out many objects.

Two P-47s strafed some German planes on the runway a couple of minutes before we hit it. The entire field was devastated. A few bombs hit the runway.

We carried 100 pound bombs and they were too small to follow all the way down. The first group started a fire that burned like thermite. It was real hot white flame. I could not figure out what it could be. There was light flak over the target.

P-47s were giving us area coverage in and out of the target. It was fairly cloudy.

I noticed a couple of battleships or destroyers by an island in the channel. I couldn't tell whether they were firing at us or shelling the island. I saw numerous flashes in the channel from smaller craft. I guess they were shelling the island because I never saw any flak.

We let down to 6,000 feet, then down to 2,000 over England. A B-24 came back with us but left us over the channel.

Bomb load – 36 – 100 lb. Anti-Personnel

CONCHES, FRANCE
11 June 1944

Our target was an airfield two miles from Bauyex. This was undoubtedly the most fouled up mission I have ever been on. We were to bomb visually but the target was cloudy. We never had a P.F.F. ship. We made five bomb runs on the target and never hit it. We were just using the sky for a playground.

We were sure lucky the Luftwaffe's didn't hit us. There were some MEs (Messerschmitts) -109s up but our escort of P-47s and P-51s kept them away. The ME109s was the primary Luftwaffe fighter at the outbreak of the war and one of the most famous fighter planes in history. It was the primary defensive aircraft against Allied bombers. They finally gave up trying to bomb and we headed back for the base. The MEs were designed in the mid-1930s, the ME 109 was the primary Luftwaffe fighter at the outbreak of the war and one of the most famous fighter planes in history. It was the primary defensive aircraft against Allied bombers.

The Navigator said we were over the channel so I dozed off in the turret. The first thing I knew I could hear flak popping in my ears and I woke up and we were over Guennsay Island at 5,000 feet. They were throwing up flak, machine gun fire, tracers, rocks, and anything else they had handy. Christ, what a boner!

We were supposed to go around it and the Navigator led us right over it at 5,000 feet! We were going about 140 miles per hour, the other half of the group went around it O.K.

We salvoed our bombs in the channel and missed the island completely. We got five flak holes and our #3 engine was knocked out. The formation broke up and we came back by ourselves.

It was foggy as all get out but that was no excuse for such a boner. I was playing poker until 12:10, then went out to eat and then went out to the ship.

Bomb load – 17 – 250 pound General Purpose Demolition

LILLE-HENDEVILLE, FRANCE
12 June 1944

We took off at 5:35 this morning. Our target was an airfield a few miles from Lillie. We were supposed to hit the runway but clouds were covering it so we changed it at the last minute and hit some hangers and buildings. It was a long bomb run. I couldn't see the field until I saw bombs hit.

We went over Hamburg on the way in and hit a bit of flak. They were tracking and coming too close for comfort.

We had P-51 escort giving us area coverage. There were a lot of planes in the air today. We also saw a lot of vessels on the English coast. An ME-109 and a F.W.-190 followed us back but never attacked.

Guess I'll hit the sack (bunk bed)!

Bomb load – 18 – 250 lb General Purpose Demolition

BRETIGNY, FRANCE
14 June 1944

Our target was an airfield 25 miles southwest of Paris. We hit it at 23,000 feet. The bomb run was 18 minutes long and we had flak all the time. That is a little too much flak to digest for so long a time. I really sweated until the bombs were gone. Flak was deadly accurate today.

I think there was a German B-17 (probably a captured American B-17) with us today giving them the altitude we were flying, etc. There was a B-17 at 2 o'clock level out about one-half mile or so. When flak started coming up he banked away from it. He never had any engines out that I could see or nothing wrong with him. When we finally got to the French coast he turned around and headed up along the coast.

We were to hit the runway and we did a damn good job. A piece of flak hit my turret on the ammunition cover. It just dented it and glanced off. We got quite a bit of flak in the waist and they pulverized the wings. Both wing tips have to be changed.

We got lots of friendly fighters up today.

Bomb load – 28 – 100 lb Demolition

NANTES, FRANCE
15 June 1944

Well, the more we fly the less chance I think we have of getting our 30 missions. Our target was a railway bridge. We had a 15 minute bomb run and bombed at 20,000 feet.

Flak was coming up when we hit the I.P. (Initial Point). That bridge must have really been militarily important. Flak guns were all over even on the other side of the river.

I saw more flashes on the ground than I've ever seen. There were so many I thought they were bomb bursts. About a minute before bombs away my oxygen was shot out. I thought that we had had it. I heard the oxygen escaping and my warning light went on so I got out of the turret and went into the radio room.

Grayson was using the left side so I connected up on the right. It was shot out so I went on a bottle for air for a few minutes and then used the line on the left side. Grayson went back to the waist and put his parachute on.

There was a hole in the wall about 18 inches long and

3 inches wide. Holes were all over the right side. Just as I stepped in the radio room the floor boards were blown off. I thought a piece of plane had come up through and burst in the radio room.

We got a few holes in the nose, too. A piece went through Carlson's helmets and through his ear phones and into his ear. It's a good thing for him he was superstitious and wore two flak helmets. He's in the hospital now. I do not know how bad it is.

Number 2 engine was hit and we nursed it along as long as we could, then we feathered it. We held formation until we got to the field, then we broke off and landed first.

We went over the invasion coast on the way in. There were a lot of ships in the harbor and convoys coming in but we were too high for me to see any action.

I saw Caen or smoke from there. Our ship (plane) was 547 put it in the hospital. We put ship 402 in there yesterday. A ship a day. Our luck can't last much longer. Somebody is going to get it or all of us. Clint is grounded for good now. We are up for tomorrow too.

Bomb load – 12 – 500 lb. Demolition

CRETUIAL, FRANCE
19 June 1944

The target today was a gun emplacement. 10/10 (100%) cloud coverage was so that I couldn't see anything. We never had a P.F.F. plane so we brought our bombs back. While I was getting in my turret my oxygen line came loose just as I was ready to run it down. We were at 20,000 so I began feeling the effects in a hurry. I rolled my turret back up and threw the door open and then started poking for the hole to make the connection. I got it connected just as I was going under. Everything was turning blue.

The target was six miles from St. Omer in the Pas de Calais area. Bombing altitude was at 25,000. We are going up again tomorrow. Gas load is 2400 – long and rough. I hope it isn't Berlin.

The High Squadron got some flak so we got credit. We took off about 6:50 and got back about 11:15.

Bomb load – 38 – 100 lb Demolition

HAMBURG, GERMANY
20 June 1944

We hit an oil plant today. We dropped on the deputy lead and his racks were out so he dropped early. We mowed down a wheat field. The flak was heavy over the target but we only got two holes.

We lost 1,000 feet going over the target. We bombed at 25,000. We went over the North Sea and then down.

Bomb load – 12 – 500 lb General Purpose Demolition

BERLIN, GERMANY
21 June 1944

Well, I have 15 missions in now and 15 missions to go. It is going to be a long tough grind if we ever do make it. Over 1,000 planes went out today and 900 Lanks (Lancaster British Bombers) were going but they were scrubbed. These British four-engine heavy bombers designed and built by Avro for the Royal Air Force, it first saw active service with the RAF Bomber Command in 1942, and became the main heavy bomber used. The "Lanc", as it was affectionately called, thus became the most famous and most successful of the Second World War night bombers. I guess they figured they would never get back … or else they would screw us up unless they came in after we did. Boy, I sure wish they would have come; maybe we wouldn't have to go there again for awhile.

We took the North Sea route and passed Hamburg on the way in. It was still burning from yesterday. There was a pall of smoke covering the entire city.

We bombed at 26,400 feet. Flak was intense but it was above us. They were throwing up that white stuff today. Two Forts collided just outside of Berlin before we dropped our bombs. One broke up and hit a P-51 on the way down. The other one went down in a flat spin. He was really turning. He came out of it partially once but couldn't make it. Another B-17 went down over Berlin.

There weren't many parachutes from any but quite a few Forts went down.

If I don't get some sleep I'll be out for awhile myself. This getting up at 12:30 every night is ruining me. We're up again tomorrow.

Bomb load – 8 – 500 lb General Purpose Demolition; 2 – 500 lb Incendiaries

ST. OMER, FRANCE (south of Calais)

22 June 1944

This was another crapped up mission! It was partly cloudy over the target. The lead Bombardier could not synchronize his sight so we made five passes at the target and never dropped our bombs. We made the same pattern at the same level over and there were some flak guns on every run. Every ship (plane) got hit. There were only a few flak guns down there but they sure should have picked off a couple of us. We only got six or seven holes at 25,000.

We had a nice big airfield for a secondary target; for some reason we never hit it. We were told to pick out our own secondary. I noticed a big building with a red cross painted on the top so that may have been why we never hit it.

We got some flak on the way in from Dunkirk. Our target was rocket gun installations between Eypres and St. Omer.

Bomb load – 6 – 500 lb Demolition

BREMEN, GERMANY
24 June 1944

Well, today was quite a day. Our target was an oil refinery just on the outskirts of town. We were first over the target but we were bombing P.F.F. so I didn't see the hits. The flak was intense and I was sure sweating the bombs out. They came out in spurts and one came out about a half-minute late. I was going to tell Grayson to be sure and check the bomb bays because one came out late. Just as I was going to call him up he said they were all gone so I never said anything.

Neimy called for a crew check and Grayson said that he was hit but it wasn't too bad. Later he looked in the bomb bay and noticed that one of them had not gone out. I went up and took a look to see if there was any danger of it falling on the doors or going off. It was O.K. though. The bomb release lever had been bent and the Bomb Shackle Release lever wasn't engaged in it.

When we got over the North Sea I went up and dropped the bomb out and took a look at Grayson's arm. A piece of flak had come through the bomb bay door and up through the radio room. It had come through with such force that it knocked some splinters off the wall and through Grayson's flying suit. Every time he moved his arm the splinters would prick him and consequently he thought it was pretty bad. I pulled the splinters out and he was O.K. other than his arm was bruised a bit.

We had a beautiful escort over the target, mostly P-38's, and all the way back.

Bombed at 25,000 feet.

Bomb load – 18 – 250 .lb Demolition

AUXERRE, FRANCE
25 June 1944

Another screwed up mission! We had some odd-ball Colonel leading us. Our target was a bridge and there was a town just on the other side of it which we didn't want to hit. First we headed for the wrong bridge but I guess the guy woke up so we

cut off and went around.

We made another pass at the target but another group had hit it so we closed our doors and looked for another target. It didn't look to me like that bridge had been hit. I saw about five holes to the left of the bridge on the edge of the town. They were near misses. A large fire was burning where the bombs had hit. We never saw a single flak burst on that target.

Next we picked on an airfield that had a million bomb holes around it. Some hangers had been hit and a damn good job was done. The dust from those 2,000 pounders rose to about 5,000 feet. I couldn't see the target until the bombs started exploding.

Our gas was running low so we jettisoned the ammunition out of the tail. When we got over the channel we broke formation and came back on our own.

The pattern over the field was busy as hell but we got in O.K.

Our target was about 50 miles south of Paris. We bombed at 17,000 feet. The name of the target was BOMILLY-SUR-SEINE.

Bomb load 2- 2,000 lb Demolition

LEIPZIG, GERMANY
29 June 1944

It was pretty good today but I was sweating a little bit. The target was an aircraft assembly plant. We led the low group and took the overland route. The temperature was 30° below. The whole mission took 8 hours, 40 minutes.

I saw a balloon barrage over a dam but that was the only unusual thing that I noticed.

Just before we opened our bomb bay door an ME 109 (Messerschmitt) made a pass at us. His only purpose was to break up our formation because I don't think he fired except at the high group as he came through. He went over the top of us so I never did see him.

A couple of ME-109s got together at 6 o'clock after that pass but left after a while.

We dropped our bombs but the right rack didn't release for a minute or so. The bomb bay door safety switch wasn't completely opened. We bombed at 26,400 feet and the flak was very moderate.

We hit the North Sea and let down to 500 feet and then 300. We didn't get any flak holes at all.

Bomb load – 500 lb demolition

MUNICH, GERMANY
11 July 1944

Well, we finally got in another mission. We had a long layoff and we had a 48 hour pass during that time.

There are a lot of rumors going around about sending this group out and the way things are going it would not surprise me. We're either standing down or we just aren't alerted and the other fields are flying.

The target today was an aircraft factory about seven miles northeast of Munich. We flew lead ship in the high element of the lead squadron. We expected fighters today because they have been sending up everything including ME-110 and 410 lately. But we never saw any fighters and most surprising of all, no flak.

We were supposed to bomb visually, if not visual, we were supposed to bomb Munich P.F.F. We hit the primary P.F.F. It was a 9 hour and 15 minute mission.

Boy was I tired! There were more planes in the air today

than on D-Day, I believe. We had 47's, 51's, and 38's for escorts.

Bomb load – 15 – 250 lb General Purpose Demolition

MUNICH, GERMANY
13 July 1944

One thousand one hundred (1,100) planes hit Munich the 11th of July. One thousand two hundred (1,200) hit it yesterday, the 12th, and I don't know how many hit it today – about 750, I think. We hit the town today P.F.F.

The flak was intense, worse than I have ever seen it, even over Berlin. We only had about four flak holes though and we were very lucky. We went over the north side of Brussels on the way in and got some flak from there.

We bombed at 25,600 feet and flew lead low squadron of the high group. We went down by Switzerland on the way over and saw the Alps. They were about level with us so they have risen to about 23,000 feet.

Fighters attached to the group behind us and I guess they hit them pretty hard. Some B-17s got panicky and was hollering he was on fire and bandits were attacking. A fighter pilot told him to take it easy, they were coming.

We had P-51s for escort and P-38s after the target. The mission took 9.02 hours. 10/10 clouds were over England and the formation broke up letting down. Visibility was less than 500 feet. Times such as this are what make a young guy old. I sure sweated out coming in. The sky was full of planes passing all over but we couldn't see them until they were right on us. One ship landed and the landing gear collapsed. Another had his rudder controls out and taxied into another ship (plane).

I met John in Northampton last night. He was staggering up the street with his engineer and I was heading for the trucks to take me back to base. It was about 10 to 11. He came up bumming me for a cigarette and he asked me about five times before he finally recognized me. I found out where he was stationed though. None of the crew got up this morning and they had to come up and get us.

Bomb load – 4 – 500 lb General Purpose Booby Traps
6 – 500 lb Incendiaries

MUNICH, GERMANY
16 July 1944

Well, today was full of events. We were never fed this morning. They said they were supposed to feed so many men and they had fed them. We were just out of luck. No C.S. (chicken shit) overseas it says here in real small print. It didn't bother me because flying kills my appetite but it was sure rough on some of the boys.

Munich was it again. Nothing happened on the way in until we hit the I.P. There was a front over the target, so we were told to climb another 2,000 feet. So we did and we were still in fog.

The formation broke up and we kept climbing. We finally got out of it at 32,000 feet. We couldn't find the formation. We'd see a few planes for a few seconds and then lose them again. Another plane at 5 o'clock about half-a-mile back was being attacked by a fighter. We watched them and then the fighter went down through the clouds. I don't know if anybody got him or he ran out of oxygen. The B-17 pulled up to us for mutual protection and it turned out to be Harrington in ship 978. He had a fire on his right wing so he didn't come in too close. A guy bailed out of the waist door and I watched him as he went down. His parachute opened just before he hit the clouds at about 15 or 16,000 feet. We were approximately at 23,000 feet. Later, two more bailed out. They pulled a good delayed jump and went down through the clouds. The first guy sure fell funny, just like a dummy. He was turning over and his legs and arms were flopping every which way. I think he must have been unconscious.

I was sure glad to see his parachute open. No others came out. We flew on for awhile, and then they turned off and headed for Switzerland. Nothing visual was wrong so I think they made it ok unless they got hit by more fighters. The fire on the wing had evidently blown itself out.

We kept on and sighted a wing (another group of B-17s) behind us so we turned around and went back and joined them. Boy, we were sure covered with luck. A lot of the other boys were attacked by fighters but none of the fighters bothered us at all.

One of the ball turret boys passed out and the radio man went back to help him and he passed out as well. Finally, Tex revived both of them. Then five fighters jumped them. The door came off of the turret and they had to crank Smitty out. He was so scared he just sat there and I don't blame him. They couldn't get the turret all the way up on account of the door. Smitty couldn't even talk!

We kept with the formation until the G box (navigational aid giving the location) was working, then headed for the English coast. We got a field on the radio and he gave us permission to land. It was about eight miles away. We were circling a field that we thought that was the one. So, we made our approach and landed. It turned out to be a condemned bomber base and the guys didn't have a radio to contact us. We were out of gas though, so it's a good thing we did or we would have flown along on an empty tank.

We got some gas from the field but our air cooler was out of order and there was oil all over the wing. We took a vote on whether we should chance it back to the base or have them fly the ground crew over and fix it. We decided on the latter.

I for one didn't want to try and stretch our luck any further for the day. They flew Johnson, the crew chief, and a few other guys over and they fixed it. We stayed there overnight and threw a party. Everybody had a few drinks, even the ground crew; that is, all but Neimy. We had a few beers on the base and then we got a truck and went to a small pub a few miles from there and had a few more beers and a couple shots of gin. They closed the place up so we went back to the base. There was just a skeleton crew of English. Also two Red Cross girls were there. One of the boys was hitting it off pretty good with one of the girls and she had an amazing memory for numbers. She knew the phone number of every base in England!

Jeff got pretty angry and he started telling Hedrick off about sucking around with Neimy. We all got a big kick out of it but I thought it best to take Jeff out and walk him around a bit. We went over to the next barracks which was full of Brits and the Colonel of the field or whatever they have was trying to tell us to go back to the barracks. He was in his undershirt and so we thought he was just another Joe so we went around and we went in. They found out how we came to be there and they loaded us down with a round block of cheese and everything we took it all back to the barracks and gave it to Carlson. He got a hell of a kick out of it. Jeff had to go to the can (toilet) all night and he'd come back in and couldn't find his bed. He always ended up in Neimy's. He'd sit on his bed and Neimy would tell him to get off and go to his own bed. Poor Jeff. He'd try to crawl in with Neimy and Neimy would kick him out.

Twelve planes went down in the channel. Everybody was short as hell on gas. They were running out on the runway. Our squadron lost two, Harrington and Huttle.

We flew back to base this morning. They had a milk run today, too. We salvoed our bombs some place in Germany.

Bomb load – 10 – 500 lb Demolition

PEENEMUNDE, GERMANY
18 July 1944

We had an important target today Germany's leading experimental station for all their new weapons and was Germany's submarine base The last time it was hit was in 1942 by the Royal Air Force (R.A.F.) Most of Germany's leading scientists were killed. They were developing rockets mainly at the time. S-27 (British Intelligence Unit) had just learned about it. It was a shame to kill all those brilliant men but it is either them or us. I'm anxious to hear the results of today's raid. It's been two years since it was hit so they may have figured it safe by now. I guess the Germans are working on robot bombs.

The target was way up in Northwestern Germany. We crossed the North Sea and the Baltic Sea. We passed Sweden 33 miles off the shore line; we could see it at 9 o'clock.

It was a 9-1/2 hour mission. We were on oxygen about 4-1/2 hours. We bombed at 24,000. Our #3 engine was vibrating and smoking on the way in. The target was visual and I could see about 10 flak guns firing at us. It was moderate but accurate as hell. We only got a couple of holes.

We plastered the target and blew up something. The flames from whatever it was came up to about 3,000 feet. There was a channel of water between two bodies of land there and they had their guns on both sides of the channel.

Some nincompoop dropped a 1,000 pound bomb on another B-17 and it went right on through taking the navigator along. Two more B-17s collided but they were all in another group though. We had a terrible formation ourselves. I'll sure be glad to finish up. There are too many new crews now and they can't fly. We flew lead, low group. We are up for Deputy Lead tomorrow. (Deputy Lead is the second plane in command. If the lead plane is shot down or disabled, Deputy Lead would then take over the lead position.)

Bomb load – 10 – 500 lb Demolition

KOTTEN, GERMANY
20 July 1944

We flew deputy lead today and Daniels aborted just before the I.P. so we took over the lead. We had a Chinese bombardier in Carlson's place. It was clear all the way until we hit the I.P. then there was just enough haze so we couldn't bomb.

We went around and made another run and that one was too short so we went around again. The third time we dropped our bombs, but by that time I figured we were overdoing it so I got out of my turret after the second run and put on my parachute. Flak over the target seemed to be intense but the majority of the reports says it was moderate. Maybe I was seeing double but it looked bad enough to me to make me get out of the ball.

The target was an airplane engine factory making engines for the new D.O. 219 reputed to be capable of 500 miles per hour (M.P.H.) It was in the vicinity of Leipzig. (This could be the Heinkel 219 as I was not familiar enough with German aircraft. I was probably told it was a Dornier 219.) On the way in #3 engine was smoking and vibrating but it stopped after awhile. Our bombing altitude was 25,600 feet.

My heated pants and shoes didn't work and it was 34 degrees below zero so my feet were pretty damn cold with just those everyday socks and thin shoes.

We had a different radio operator, a 10-mission man. I guess he's a hot rock and they want to break him in for lead.

We went through Ruhr Valley on the way in. Neimy and Chun are up for the D.F.C. (Distinguished Flying Cross).

The papers say 30 ME-410s were ready to jump us

yesterday about 4,000 feet above us and some P-51s jumped them and knocked out 21 of them. I was wondering why we never hit fighters.

Bomb load – 10 – 500 lb. General Purpose Demolition

EBELSBACH, GERMANY
21 July 1944

Well, we're right up there in lead now. They scratched Daniels and put us in the lead. We had two pilots and also had Chun for a bombardier. Resser is getting way behind. I've only got eight more to go now.

We formed at 11,000 feet. We hit a front just before the I.P. The target was smoked over and Chun missed it and bombed god only knows what. There was no flak over the target but we were getting it thrown up in and out of the target. None reached us. Some was tracking the low group though. (Groups few at different altitudes. Lead group: high group and low group.)

Bomb load – 10 – 500 General Purpose Demolition
1 – Smoke bomb

MERSEBURG, GERMANY
28 July 1944

An 8-hour mission is on for today. We hit it previously on 12 May 1944. It's a synthetic oil plant, the largest in Germany. I really sweated this one out because we had John for pilot. He's a converted co-pilot and how in the hell he even made co-pilot I can't understand. He can't fly for a damn.

All the way we crossed over the low squadron back and

forth, back and forth, with only 500 feet in between us. Every time I thought sure as hell we were going to hit them. The low squadron was flying too high and John just wouldn't climb up any higher.

I saw smoke bomb trails from the group ahead of us over the target but couldn't see any flak. It was way ahead of us and it took us a long time to get there. You can see a long way above the clouds.

We almost collided with another plane just after bombs away. We were crossing over the low squadron again. I didn't see it until he was right below us. Resser was telling John to watch out as we were going to hit him. Fighters were in the vicinity. Hedrick got nervous and saw two P-51s and hollered we were being attacked so John started evasive action all by ourselves. He didn't even say what time they were coming in so I didn't know where to start shooting. I sure wish to hell they'd get him off the crew.

The fighters hit the group ahead. Boy, our formation closed up in a hurry! All but us, John just couldn't hold his position. The Chaf worked beautifully today. We never got any flak over the target but they threw up a lot after we were over. We bombed P.F.F. at 25,400 feet. The target was two miles from town proper.

I also saw a convoy of barges in the Rhine River

Bomb load – 10 – 500 lb General Purpose Demolition

MERKWILLER, GERMANY
3 August 1944

Well, today was quite a day. We hit the target good,

bombed at 20,000 feet and the smoke from the target came up to 17,000 feet. On the way in we crossed through Holland. It was a beautiful day with scattered clouds all over the sky.

In Holland I saw a canal and locks; there were a lot of small craft in a waterway next to it. A bit farther on we noticed a smoke screen. I couldn't make out what they were covering.

A P-51 went down to see I guess and when he came back up a piece of flak got him or something happened. He was out at 4.30 all by himself and he just went down and exploded. (Directions are given according to the face of a clock. 12 o'clock high would be straight ahead above you. 4:30 was not quite straight behind you.)

There were a lot of B-17s hitting the target so we lined up to have at it which put us about 10 minutes behind schedule. The whole target was on fire and covered with smoke so I couldn't make out anything on the ground.

After we left the target before our new escort picked us up we were hit by eight F.W.-190s. There were some dog fights before the target and I was hoping they took care of them but they came in on our tail at 5 and 7 o'clock. Two of them were coming in at 7 o'clock and the first was going into a barrel roll.

I started firing at him and kept on as he fell below. He was as close as hell to us and I could see my tracers going into him. I kept shooting at him until his right wing broke off and I knew he wouldn't be back up. I turned my turret back up and took a few shots at the next one. He started smoking and went off in a bank.

Two B-17s were going down at 5.30 so I took a look at

them to see if any of the guys were getting out. One broke up and about seven parachutes came out. Jeff said the other one went into a dive. Anthony was in one of them. By this time the fighters were coming in again from the nose and over the top so I didn't get a chance at them. Our new escort came up and they high-tailed it off.

One P-51 was flying below us about 400 feet and the ball turret on ship 424 started firing at him. I was searching the sky for anymore fighters when I noticed his guns smoking so I wheeled my turret down to see what he was firing at and I saw this P-51. He peeled off awfully slow so I kind of think that he was hit. Then they called over the V.H.F. that somebody was shooting at a P-51.

We had a substitute pilot and he scared the hell out of us. Our right wing man hit prop wash and we damn near had it there. When we got back to the field a plane was burning on the end of the runway so we couldn't come in right away. Another one made a crash landing and the guys bailed out over the field. They got banged up landing because they were pretty low when they bailed out. The ship caught fire when it landed. The raid was about seven hours long.

Most of the guys that went down today were almost finished up. Bender had a few to go but Haan wanted to finish us today so he flew in Benders' place and went down. It looked like it would be a milk run today but it sure as hell turned out differently.

Bomb load – 20 – 250 lb General Purpose Demolition

ANKLAM, (Northwest) GERMANY
4 August 1944

We are almost done now and our missions seem to be getting rougher. Maybe it's because we're almost through and we're sweating them out more.

This mission was 9 hours, 28 minutes. It was a foggy take off although it was postponed for 30 minutes. We had good fighter escorts today.

We took the North Sea route and went down through Denmark. I noticed quite a few air fields as we came in Denmark. We got about half way across and some jet propelled planes hit the group ahead, then went around and hit the group behind. I guess we were flying pretty good formation. One guy says they look like B-26s. They made two or three passes and knocked down four B-17s. A P-51 knocked one down as it made a pass. At least our fighters can get them. I guess there were about six of them. There were nine planes leaving contrails as they passed us about 3,000 feet above us and I'm pretty sure that was them.

Our target was an FW plant. We hit it visually and hit it good. The whole 8th Air Force must have been there today. There was smoke coming from all over that place. They hit Kiel, Hamburg, Bremen and Peenemunde. As we approached land I could see them throwing up flak from different targets. They threw some at us when we got over the land but it was way off. I could see the guns firing.

I saw about 30 F.W.-190s on a field just after the target and I think some of the fighters went down and worked them over. There were a lot of 190s and 109s up today but luck was with us and the P-51s kept them away. We also saw a lot of these smoke trails today. I don't know if they were rockets or what. A B-17 was on the deck just after target; six parachutes came out. Boy, they are a long way from home.

We bombed at 18,000 feet and carried 500 pound General Purpose bombs. The other planes carried 500 pound incendiaries. Our gas load was 2,780 and we flew lead, high group. Fighters followed us out over the North Sea but never attacked. Kiel was throwing up a good smoke screen but it looked like they had some boats down there. Hamburg was smoking as we passed it on the way.

Bomb load – 10 – 500 lb General Purpose Demolition

BRETTEVILLE SUR LAIZE AREA, FRANCE
8 August 1944

I thought today would be a milk run but it turned out differently. We got up about 6:30 and we didn't have any briefing. Take off was at 10:25 and we formed at 4,000 feet. We opened our bomb bay doors in the channel and went in over the Cherbourg Peninsula.

It was cloudy and misty over the target. Our target was the German front lines. They must have wised up about using heavies to bomb the lines like that from the last time we used them because they had flak all along the lines. The flak must have stretched for 10 or 15 miles.

The flak picked us up just after the bombs away and tracked us until we were out of range which was a hell of a long time. But they were was just a little low as I could see it and hear it burst. It shook the plane with every burst.

Jeff kept telling O'Donnell that they were tracking but we couldn't do anything about it. They tracked us all over and stayed with us even on the turn. I was going to get out of the turret but it came over the V.H.F. there were fighters up so I had to stay in.

I saw more ships on the coast than I've ever seen. There was a convoy going and coming from England. The target was by Caen. Our bombs had this new explosive R.D.X. They weighed 262 pounds and were the same size as a 100 pound bomb. R.D.X. is an initalism for Research Department Explosive. It is a major 92% of C4 explosive. C4 is referred to as plastic explosive. It looks like grey clay. It can be shaped like clay. A pound looks like a pound of butter. A pound will blow up a house. A handful will blow up any door. Soldiers will take a small piece and set it on fire to cook coffee. It is also used in mining. Today was the largest bomb load ever taken off this field and we bombed at 14,000 feet. The gas load was 2,100.

Bomb load – 30 – 262 lb Anti-Personnel

MUNICH, GERMANY
9 August 1944

We bombed Old Rout 66 so much we began to think we were actually on it. Our target was the same air field where robot planes were being experimented with. We aborted this side of France. The lead ship aborted and that put the mission under a new navigator just after we had formed into our area, the son-of-a-gun! From what they say he hit all the flak there was.

They didn't hit the primary but the tank works at Stuggart and flak really knocked them out. Ship 090 went down. The radio operator had 33 missions in. All planes got hit and badly.

The high squadron leader aborted, too. They've been working these planes too hard. I'm sure glad we aborted. Flak knocked the formation out and they came back in groups of three and four. I'd be scared stiff from here on if we'd gone today. We brought our bombs back. The gas load was 2,780.

Bomb load – 500 lb Demolition

GELSENKIRCHEN, GERMANY
26 August 1944

Today we finally got in another mission. Gas load was 2,500. I was pretty glad to fly and Jeff was, too. We've been having too much time to sweat them out. We had good P-47 escort all the way to the target but after that we never saw any. We were supposed to have P-51s on the way out as well.

Our target one of the three oil refineries left in Germany. All of them were hit today so that should wind up Germany's oil.

Takeoff was postponed twice but we got off at 8:35. We bombed at 29,000 feet which was the highest we've ever bombed but it still wasn't high enough. The target was in the Ruhr Valley.

They got more flak there than in any part of Germany and god but they are good. It was rocking the plane all over and they were throwing up a lot of white flak. It must have been 155-mm stuff. I'd liked to see the guns that shoot that stuff! Boy, I was scared!

We were going right through the smoke it was so close.

As soon as we left the target all the planes in the lead element feathered a propeller; damn near at the same time.

Gas was coming out of the tank on our left wing which kept me very much on edge. I'm not afraid of getting hit by flak myself. My worry is the ship exploding, and then nobody has a chance to get out.

Well, a lot of guys straggled, had props wind-milling and feathered but we got back O.K. As we came in for a landing we had to go around. Colonel Reed came in with his brakes shot out so he used a parachute for brakes and ran off the runway. He went out in the field but made it O.K.

We landed on a flat tire and didn't know it until we were down. The shear pin broke and we ran off the runway. O'Donnell made a beautiful landing. I was still afraid of fire because of the gas on the wing. Our tail was sticking out on the runway and the next guy was coming in on three engines. They started shooting flares so he had to go around. I'll bet he was sore as hell. He had a hell of a time climbing back up with only the three engines going. We finally got pulled off the runway so the rest of them could land.

So now we have three to go! I also got a letter from the one and only which helped considerably.

Bomb load – 18 – 250 General Purpose Demolition

KIEL, GERMANY
29 August 1944

I was kind of worried about this mission but it turned out to be a milk run because the Navigator screwed up and missed the target. 10/10 clouds were over the target. We bombed P.F.F. Hannigan said we missed the target by 15 miles. There was a little flak but none bothered us. Gas load was 2,600.

We took the North Sea route, then down to Kiel. We had taken off about 1 p.m. and landed about 5:30 or 6. We bombed at 26,000 feet.

It was a lovely mission, no fighters, no trouble at all. We probably would have though if we had hit the target. Neimy and Hannigan finished up today.

Bomb load – 5 – 1,000 lb Demolition

LUDWIGSHAFEN, GERMANY
5 September 1944

The target today was an oil distillery. The weather going in was lousy. The formation almost broke up once. We led the high squadron and took them up to 22,500 feet and finally got out of the clouds. The lead element never did get up there. We saw them when it cleared off a bit so we reformed. We bombed at 25,000 feet. I didn't watch the bombs hit. The P-51s came in and looked us over all the way back and gave us good escort. Gas load was 2,600.

Flak over the target was deadly. It was a cloudy day, too. We bombed P.F.F. I guess. Flak knocked out our #1 engine right away. We couldn't feather it so it was wind milling all the way home which didn't help matters any at all. We had a hole in the gas tank and gas was leaking out all the way back. The left wing was punctured like a sieve. The #2 engine was smoking for awhile but it was the gas mixture. We fell out of formation right after the target. I have only one more mission to go.

Boy, it is sure a lot different flying over France since our boys have taken it. Nobody was shooting at us or nothing. It seemed to take a long time to cross it today though. O'Donnell made a beautiful landing.

Some ball turret got a direct hit. A few got wounded today, I guess. I'm sure glad I got it in though; only I got one to go now.

Bomb load – 6 – 1,000 lb Demolition

MERSBURG, GERMANY
11 September 1944

We aborted right after take off. The #4 engine was leaking oil. We thought it was gas. We feathered it but started it again for landing. It was smoking like hell so I put my parachute on and was sitting by the door waiting for somebody to make a move and I would have been gone. We were to fly deputy lead today.

Bombing altitude was 27,000 feet and carried a 2,500 gallon gas load. As we were making a turn for the approach, the sun shone on the smoke and it looked to Jeff like I was on fire and it sure scared the hell out of him. It just happened to look like it was on fire from where he was standing.

Still have one mission to go. I'm beginning to wonder if we'll ever get it in. Grayson finished up Friday. We were damn lucky we never went today; the guy that took our place went down. They got hit by 109s and 190s. The group lost 19 planes. Squadron 407 lost 13 out of 18 that went out.

We had a lot narrower escape the last raid than we knew. Fire broke out in the wing and burned the braces off the gas tank. Speaking of luck or whatever it is, a piece of flak that had gone up through the bottom of the tank and right up through the gas cap knocking the cap off. Because of that no fumes collected in the wing, otherwise we would have blown up. Flak tore the bottom of the tank out and all the wires were burnt out, too.

Bomb load – 10 – 500 lb. General Purpose Demolition

TACTICAL: HOLLAND
17 September 1944

This is a briefing to achieve our goal. I have finally finished up. It was a wonderful milk run. I flew with some guy named Joe! He was really a poor pilot. Our #4 amplifier went out on the take off and we were in some prop wash. We used all the runway we had and I still didn't think we would make it. We bombed at 9:44 and carried these R.D.X. bombs – 262 pounds each. God, but they are powerful. I could see the concussions when they exploded. We bombed at 18,000 feet but I could not see or make out anything on the ground.

I never saw any flak at all but there was some to the left. I saw four parachutes at the I.P. but didn't see the burning B-17 that they came out of. I don't know how he went down either. He was way up ahead of us but Carlson saw him.

We bombed gun installations in Holland. We were in

formations of six planes. There were a lot of planes up today. The channel was also full of convoys coming and going.

On the way back we passed the C-47s and gliders that took the boys in that invaded Holland today. We were bombing in support of them.

We circled England for two hours.   Landingwasrough and pretty bad. I got kind of sick today as we were coming in. and we were flying pretty rough. I was pretty high strung anyway. We got up at 2:20 and took off at 6:05. The gas load was 2,200 gallons.

Bomb load – 30 – 262 lb Anti-personnel

CHAPTER 3
MY MISSIONS

1. Berlin   5-4-44
   (Berlin   Aborted)
2. Merseburg   5-12-44
3. Stettin   5-13-44
4. Berlin   5-19-44
5, Saarbrucken   5-23-44
6. Cottbus   5-29-44
7. Longues   6-6-44
8. Lorient-Herlin- Bastard 6-7-44
9. Conches   6-11-44
10. Lille-Hendeville   6-12-77
11, Bretigny   6-14-44
12. Nantes, Frnace   6-15-44
13. Cretuial, France   6-19-44
14. Hamburg   6-20-44
15. Berlin   6-21-44
16. St. Omer   6-22-44
17. Bremen   6-24-44
18. Auxerre   6-25-44
19. Leipzig   6-29-44
20. Munich   7-11-44
21. Munich   7-13-44
22. Munich   7-16-44
23. Peenemunde   7-18-44

24. Kotten	7-20-44
25. Ebelbach	7-21-44
26. Merseberg	7-28-44
27. Merkwiller	8-3-44
28. Anklam	8-4-44
29. Bretteville	8-8-44

Sur Laizse Area

30. Munich	8-9-44
31. Gelsenkirchen	8-26-44
32. Kiel	8-29-44
33. Ludwigshafen	9-5-44
34. Merseburg	9-11-44
35. Tactical-Holland	9-17-44

Additional 17 flights were not technically called missions. We flew up and down the Channel relaying radio transmissions from the group to base and back. It was called cycle relay. We did not carry any bombs or approach any target, but if any German fighters were out looking for something to do, we were an easy target.

Hank's Gallery

Hank with his crew. He is standing in the back, first
man on the left (facing the camera)

Age 22, after returning home from the war.

Hunched down by the ball turret.

In front of a restored B-17(Sentimental Journey)
at Joint Base McCord. He was given a flight and
an autographed picture of the plane from all the crew.

Examples of the B-17 Fying Fortress

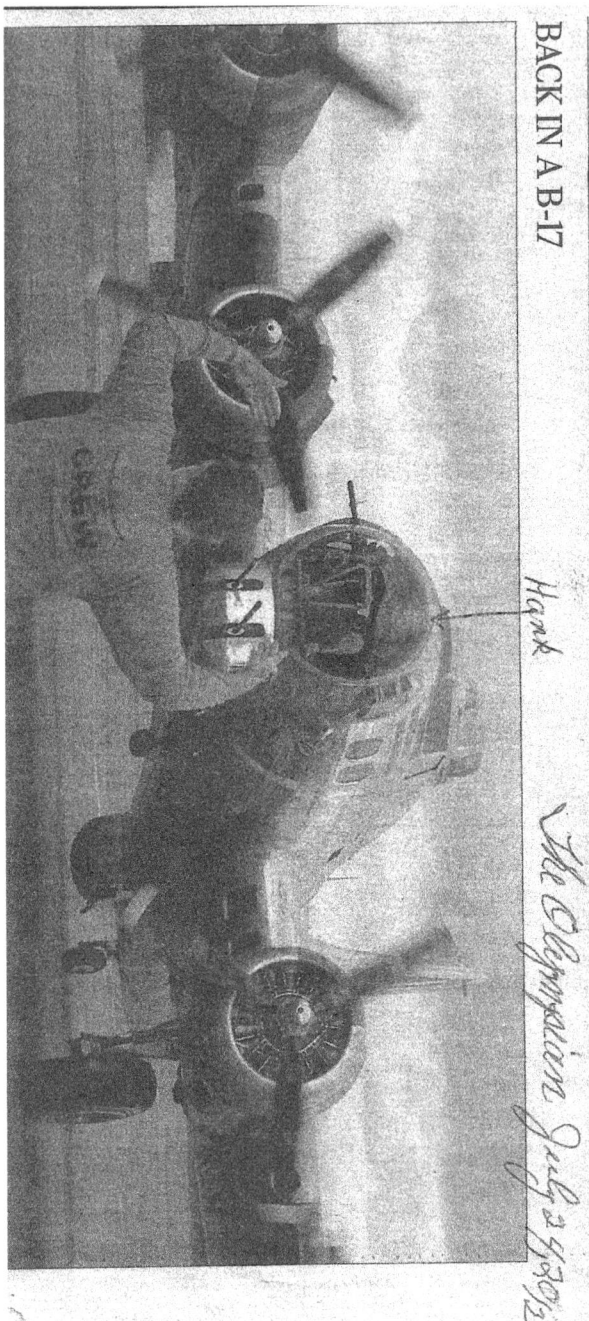

BACK IN A B-17

Hank

The Olympians July 24, 2012

Enjoying a bird's eye view from the bombardier's seat, 89-year old World War II veteran and Spanaway resident Henry Smith arrives with the crew of The Sentimental Journey, a Boeing B-17G bomber that flew into the Olympia airport on a cloudy Monday morning from the Joint Base Lewis McChord. Smith served on similar B-17s in Europe as a ball turret gunner from 1944 to 1945, and the morning's flight was a gift from his family and a sentimental journey for himself. This B-17 was put into service on March 13 ,1945, and although manufactured too late to see action in Europe, saw service in the Pacific theatre for the duration of the war. It is powered by four Wright Cyclone radial engines, which each develop 1,200 horsepower to give a top speed of more than 280 mph. The Sentimental Journey will be available at the Olympic Flight Museum for tours and rides through July 30. Flight information can be obtained by calling 602-448-9415. (do not call)

STEVE BLOOM/northwood timeswords

Enjoying a bird's-eye view from the bombardier's seat, 89-year-old World War II veteran and Spanaway resident Henry Smith arrives with the crew of The Sentimental Journey, a Boeing B-17G bomber that flew into the Olympia Airport on a cloudy Monday morning from Joint Base Lewis-McChord. Smith served on similar B-17s in Europe as a ball-turret gunner from 1944 to 1945, and the morning's flight was a gift from his family and a sentimental journey for himself. This B-17 was put into service on March 13, 1945, and although manufactured too late to see action in Europe, saw service in the Pacific theater for the duration of the war. It is powered by four Wright Cyclone radial engines, which each develop 1,200 horsepower to give a top speed of more than 280 mph. The Sentimental Journey will be available at the Olympic Flight Museum for tours and rides through July 30. Flight information can be obtained by calling 602-448-9415

The Journal of the San Juan Islands | SanJuanJournal.com

OPINION

Wednesday, May 26, 2010 — 7

Ferry Home Companion

May 8: V-E Day at the World War II Memorial

Howard Schonberger
Columnist

Talk about double whammy.

V-J Day at the American Legion in March was a fund-raiser for the veterans who wanted to take the inaugural Honor Flight from Seattle to see the newest war memorial for World War II veterans in D.C.

This writer and his wife, Helen Sawyer, won a free dinner at The Bluff for doing an Army version of "The Kiss" photo taken on Times Square at the war's conclusion.

Since I had gone through OCS with Sen. Bob Dole, who helped the fund-raising drive to build that monument, I decided it would be a kick to be among the thousands of vets he has greeted since the memorial's completion a few years ago.

Thousands of WWII vets die each week. Now, veterans and non-veterans, often children and grandchildren of vets, are pitching in with veterans organizations like the

Legion, VFW, service clubs and USO to comprise 96 "hubs" that send groups to spend a Saturday in the nation's capital.

Jim Broe — executive director of Freedom Fighters Honor Flight, a Vietnam War vet whose father was a WWII vet — leads a host of volunteers. Five guardians, including a nurse, accompanied this first group of 10 vets and the volunteers paid their own way. Southwest Airlines picked up the travel costs, as it does for other distant hubs requiring air travel (Honor Flight pays for veterans' stays at the Beltway Hilton in Baltimore).

Last year, Broe and Legion and VFW posts in Seattle decided it was time for Western Washington to match the Eastern hub in Spokane. "These trips serve as a reminder to these veterans that their past service so long ago is not forgotten."

Does it ever.

I was surprised to be the

only one from our county (two couples). A few of the guys grumbled: "Just like the Army — hurry up and wait." We were given our boarding passes and introduced to our guardians. One guy said, "I haven't had a guardian since I was in kindergarten." Then we were whisked to security (I

duced to our guardians. One guy said, "I haven't had a guardian since I was in kindergarten." Then we were whisked to security (I

got to use my pacemaker for special treatment so I wouldn't set off alarms).

At the gate, we were cheered by a bunch of USO personnel and given white Honor Flight caps (so they could spot us if we went astray.) We were given great sweaters ascribed, "If you can read this, thank a teacher ... If you can read this in English, thank a veteran." At first I thought that was nasty, then I realized it was talking about having won the war against the Axis nations whose languages might well have been mandatory had they won the war.

We all sat in front on the big plane. The captain announced our presence as we finished loading and

Veterans gather at the U.S. Marine (Iwo Jima) Memorial in Washington, D.C., on the 65th anniversary of V-E Day, Journal columnist Howard Schonberger is standing, second from right.

See FLOW, Page 8

62

HONOR FLIGHT
Certificate of Recognition

Henry Smith

In recognition of your
Honor Flight to visit your
World War II Memorial on 8
May 2010.

HONOR FLIGHT

WORLD WAR II MEMORIAL

DAVE REICHERT, HONORARY CHAIRMAN

THE WINGS OF FREEDOM TOUR

Certificate for Flight Experience

PRESENTED TO

Hank Smith

The Collings Foundation sincerely
appreciates your support of the
Wings of Freedom Tour. Your flight
experience aboard our restored World
War II vintage bombers enables us to
keep our aviation heritage alive as
we fly throughout the United States.
Thank you for your donation to help
"keep 'em flying" for the benefit of all.

THE COLLINGS FOUNDATION

This certificate is good for a Flight Experience aboard the B-24 Liberator
or the B-17 Flying Fortress. Issued on June 1, 2010. ra

Hank with his Honor Flight friend.

Remembering.

THE HEROISM OF OUR OWN TROOPS...WAS MATCHED BY THAT OF THE ARMED FORCES OF THE NATIONS THAT FOUGHT BY OUR SIDE... THEY ABSORBED THE BLOWS AND THEY SHARED TO FULL IN THE ULTIMATE DESTRUCTION OF THE ENEMY.

Sentimental Journey
Commemorative Air Force Arizona Wing Aviation Museum

71

Chapter 4
Puget Sound Honor Flight

On 12 April 2010, I was selected, along with 12 other veterans, to fly to Washington, D.C. on the Inaugural Honor flight of the Freedom Fighters to visit the World War II Memorial, all expenses paid. They also expressed an interest in my diary of missions during the war as ball turret gunner aboard a B-17.

We landed at the Baltimore Airport and were bused to the Hilton Hotel where we were assigned to our rooms. I shared a room with Howard Schonberger, a columnist marketing representative for the San Juan Island Journal. Howard lives in Friday Harbor, Washington. We had that industry in common as I had been a pressman for the Tacoma News Tribune in the 50's.

The rest of the day we boarded the bus and toured sections of Washington, D.C., then the World War II Memorial, which was inspiring to say the least.

At the statue of the raising of the American flag at Iwo Jima we were told to look at it from every point as we circled its base. The flag appeared as though it were being raised as we moved from point to point.

The Vietnam Memorial was next, where Max Bettman, my wheelchair pilot searched for a comrade's name on the Wall. I was immensely impressed by the Air Force Memorial with its three stainless steel spires soaring skyward. This was the experience of a lifetime and I am grateful to the Honor Flight for giving me and other veterans the opportunity.

Everyone wanted to shake our hands and thank us for serving our country. We were treated like heroes in every respect. When we returned home to Seattle we were greeted by applauding well-wishers, waving flags and cheering us on. Congressman Dave Reichert, our Washington State Legislator and other dignitaries ushered us into the USO Room and presented each vet with a framed certificate and a commemorative engraved coin as well as a royal USO supper. I had a great time.

Veterans from all over the United States will be honored and given the same opportunity as I to visit the World War II Memorials in Washington, D.C., because of the "Freedom Fighters Honor Flight" and a great bunch of people, whom to just say "THANKS" doesn't cover it, but "THANKS!:

When I arrived home there was an email from Keith Eldridge of KOMO TV. He and a photographer came to the house. The interview was featured that evening on the 4 and 6 o'clock news. An article in the News Tribune came out the following Sunday. Keith also informed me that a couple had seen his interview with him and wanted to sponsor a flight for Hank in a B-17 that was scheduled to fly out of Boeing Field in June. The gentleman who offered this flight to me was Colonel Mike Selk. I would be flying with him and his crew to Olympia.

On 25 July 2012, I attended an air show of Joint Base McChord with my son-in-law, John, and grandson, Twe. On display was a B-17 bomber with all its crew. When the Crew Chief, Colonel Mike Walters found out that I had been a ball turret gunner in World War II, he wanted to hear about it. He asked me if I would be interested in flying with them the following Monday to Olympia where their next showing was scheduled. Come Monday, I took my second B-17 flight, but this time I rode in the nose where the nose gunner sits. The crew took photos and presented him with a large picture, signed by all, of their plane, "Sentimental Journey" which hangs on the wall next to my computer.

On Memorial Day Hank's pastor talked a little about Hank's war service and the KOMO interview. He asked Hank to come to the podium and represent the World War II veterans and say a prayer for the many service men and women who died serving their country as well as those now serving. Hank was given a standing ovation.

On 1 October 2010, a 5-year process culminated when Joint Base Lewis-McChord reached its final operational capability and was formally established as one of 12 joint bases worldwide. Merging Fort Lewis and McChord Air Force Base, the creation of JBLM was directed as part of a 2005 Base Realignment and Closure Action. With the establishment of the joint base, all installation support functions are provided by the Army-led Joint Base Garrison to all the services on the bases – Army, Air Force, Navy, and Marines.

Chapter 5
Honor Flight
Network

The Honor Flight honors all veterans; first it was only for World War II veterans. However, inasmuch as so many of them are passing on to their "greater glory," it is now also for the Korean and Vietnam veterans.

The Honor Flight Network program was conceived by Earl Morse, a physician's assistant and a Retired Air Force Captain. He wanted to honor the veterans he had taken care of for the past 27 years. After retiring from the Air Force in 1998, he was hired by the Department of Veterans Affairs to work in a small clinic in Springfield, Ohio.

In May 2004, the World War II Memorial was finally completed and dedicated in Washington, D.C., quickly becoming the topic of discussion among the World War II veterans. These veterans doubted that they would ever be able to travel to visit THEIR MEMORIAL! Many thought they just might be able to make it with a family member or friend. However, summer turned to fall and then winter. As they returned to their clinic for follow-up visits, they were asked by Earl if they had been unable to accomplish their dream. It was clear that most of them were financially or physically able for them to complete the journey. Many of them were in their 80s and lacked the ability to complete such a trip on their own. Unfortunately, family members and friends were also unable to have the resources and time to assist their veterans to make the 3 or 4 day trip to the nation's capital.

Earl knew that the majority of the veterans had given up all hope of ever visiting the memorial that was specifically created to honor their services as well as the services of their fellow comrades who had paid the ultimate sacrifice. That's when Earl decided that there had to be a way to get these heroes to D.C. to see their memorial.

In December 2004, Earl asked one of his World War II patients, "Would it be all right if I personally flew you to D.C., free of charge, to visit the patient's memorial?" Mr. Loy broke down and cried. He told Earl that at his age he would probably never get to see his memorial otherwise and graciously accepted the offer.

Earl posed the same question to a World War II veteran a week later. He too cried and enthusiastically accepted the trip. It didn't take long for Earl to realize that there were many veterans who would have the same reaction. So he started asking for help from other pilots to make these dreams a reality. In January 2005, Earl addressed about 150 members of the Aero Club during a safety meeting, outlining a volunteer program to fly veterans to their memorial.

There were two major stipulations to his request. The first was that the veterans pay nothing. The entire aircraft rental ($600 to $1200 for the day) would have to be paid solely by the pilots. The second was that the pilots personally escort the veterans around D.C. for the entire day.

After Earl spoke, eleven pilots who had never met his patients stepped up to volunteer. And the Honor Flight was born!

Soon other dedicated volunteers joined, a board was formed, funds were raised and the first flight took to the air in May 2005. Six small planes flew 12 very happy veterans to Manassas, Virginia; just outside of Washington, D.C. Vans transported the pilots and veterans into D.C. and to the World War II Memorial. The responses from both the veterans and the pilots were overwhelming. It was an experience that will remain with them for the rest of their lives. Soon other flights were planned and made. So many veterans wanted to participate that commercial airlines were used to accommodate forty veterans at a time, including many in wheelchairs. By the end of the first year, Honor Flight had transported 137 World War II veterans to their memorial.

In 2006, commercial flights were exclusively used due to the number of veterans on the waiting list; adverse weather conditions which prohibited small aircraft from participating on a regular schedule. Another 300 veterans participated during that year!

The mission and ideals of the program began to spread across America. Other cities and states became aware of our efforts and we fostered working relationships with dedicated community leaders in several states. Jeff Miller, Hendersonville, North Carolina, led the expansion into areas not serviced by direct commercial flights to the Washington, D.C. area. He accomplished what was thought to be impossible, organizing and obtaining funding to fly an entire commercial jet filled with local veterans to visit the memorial.

We are proud to say that (1) all of our heroes had a safe and memorable trip and (2) we were able to raise sufficient funds so that every veteran flew absolutely free

24 September 2007, Honor Air out of Hendersonville, NC and Henderson County, NC were the first city and the first county in the nation to fly 100% of their World War II veterans to their memorial.

In May 2008, Southwest Airlines stepped up by donating thousands of free tickets, and was named the official commercial carrier of the Honor Flight Network in a joint press release. It is because of this generous donation that the Honor Flight Network undoubtedly has more flexibility, more opportunity, and are now more than ever able to serve more veterans on our "anxiously waiting list" would have been possible given the economy and the decrease in charitable donations.

There is a network of participating programs in place to assist our senior heroes. Resources are pooled, experience is shared and alliances are formed throughout America to get our World War veterans to their memorial safely.

The Honor Flight Network presently has 127 hubs in 41 states. Due to the senior age of our heroes and all within our power to make their dream a reality and the prediction that we are losing 800 of them daily, we are committed to do all within our power to make their dream a reality. Our current focus will remain on World War II heroes and those veterans from any other war who have a terminal illness. However, our vision goes beyond World War II. They, too, have given so much and it's time we show them that their efforts are not forgotten. Honor Flight Network has learned a lot over the last few years and one point that stands out is that our veteran heroes aren't asking for recognition. It is our position that they deserve it! Our program is just a small token of our appreciation for those that gave so much.

Please help us continue to make their dream of visiting THEIR memorial a reality. HONOR FLIGHT NETWORK – OUR WAY OF SAYING TO ALL OUR VETERANS – ONE MORE TOUR WITH HONOR!

It is important to recognize two of our honorary advisors, Senator Elizabeth Dole and Senator Bob Dole.

Inasmuch as the author resides in California, she is

including the regional hubs in this state. For other states, feel free to contact Honor Flight Network in Ohio.

Flying from SFO (San Francisco International, SJC (San Jose International) :

Contact Carl Stewart at 408 925-1999

John Armlenta 408 925-1999

Flying from FAT (Fresno Yosemite International)

Al Perry 559 970-9853

559 285-5975

HONOR FLIGHT CENTRAL COAST CA. INC. (PASO ROBLES)

Flying from SBP (San Luis Obispo Co. & SMX (Santa Maria Public)

805 610-4012

805 440-1551

HONOR FLIGHT KERN COUNTY HUB WEB SITE

Flying from Kern County (Bakersfield, CA)

Lil Marsh   661 303-3837

Lori Crown   661 333-1001

HONOR FLIGHT OF NORTHERN CA (ANDERSON, CA) HUB WEB SITE

Flying from SFO (San Francisco International) & SMF (Sacramento)

Debbi   530 357-3380

Tom Johnson   530 357-3380

For Puget Sound Honor Flight; contact Denise Rouleau 206 390-5830.

DONATIONS: If every adult in the country could send ONE DOLLAR ($1.00) think of how many of our heroes the HONOR FLIGHT NETWORK could take to Washington, D.C. to see their own memorials? Let's do it, folks!

ONE DOLLAR EACH PERSON!

ACKNOWLEDGMENTS

I must give Henry G. and his wife, Fay Smith, much of the credit for his story, his corrections, additions as without his input, his story would have been wanting. He should also be appreciated for his service to our country. If it were not for men like him, this country would probably not exist as it does today. We not only owe all our veterans respect but appreciate what they sacrificed in doing their duty to God, the American people, and this country. I also wish to acknowledge the fact that he and his wife, Fay, came down from Washington State to meet me, took me to a fine dinner, and a great friendship developed from this meeting. I shall forever be grateful the two of them came to my home to meet me. Fine conversations also took place.

Thanks must also be given to Michael Miles, a long-time friend of mine as is his lovely wife, Deborah ("Debbie"), who read Mr. Smith's manuscript for me. He has given of himself to me in the way of tolerating me all the way across this wonderful country with his group, Run For the Wall, when I was 71 years of age. He was always polite, kind, and helpful. This group makes this same tour every year in honor of the Vietnam veterans who never got a welcome home but for any veteran who wishes to make this wonderful journey. Debbie and I spent almost 7 years sending care packages to our troops in Afghanistan and Iraq. We had 5 troops wounded but none killed and felt very special by God that none were killed. After Mike had read the manuscript, he brought a photograph book of airplanes "back in those days" advised as well as that I should contact the Air Force Public Affairs office regarding obtaining photographs of the bombs that were used. They were of no help at all, so …

I contacted my son, Tech Sgt. M. Douglas Peterson of the United States Air Force Reserves, Fort Lewis (Army) and Camp McChord (Air Force), Washington, now called Joint Base McChord. He suggested I send him copies of what proof I had a book was actually being written, otherwise, he probably would not be able to obtain what I needed. They were sent; my son goes on weekend "warrior duty" once a month and for two weeks each year. To give you a little additional history on my son, while he was an MP with the United States Marine Corps for 5 years and wanted to change his MOS. Of course, his request was denied so he left the Marine Corps and went into the Army Reserves; didn't like them so joined the Air Force Reserves. After 2-1/2 years his entire unit was activated so he served another (approximately) 4 years on active duty. He was the hydraulics engineer and received a number of awards for his service. These were for the C-17 huge cargo planes. He was assigned to go to other countries to fill in for an Airman who wanted to take his leave home which he did. Also he was advised to get his International Driver's License and did so. When he was a Marine he served 2 years in Korea. But that's another story, another time!

Thanks should also be shared with Tom Watson, my consultant, and friend. We have been working together for approximately 8 years. He does a magnificent job in designing the front and back covers, placing the photographs where they belong, and is presently working on my 4th manuscript "What Did You Do In the Great War, Grandpa?" This one will be my largest book, and thus far the costliest. Tom is very thorough, kind, friendly, and does excellent work. He even offers me great advice from time to time, and on occasion, takes me to special meetings. Tom is better known as children's book author T.E. Watson and yet puts up with me!

To all the people, some of them neighbors, way too many to mention, have been supportive in my writings, musings, and being amazed at the "notoriety" I have achieved over the past few years. While I was working on my first POW manuscript (my 6th book), many of my neighbors would let me talk with them to vent! I continue to be in touch with many of the veterans who are listed in my books not only in correspondence but also telephone calls and email messages, and purchase of my books, my heartfelt thanks to each of you!

Bibliography

Dive Bomber –Learning to Fly the Navy's Fighter Planes, by Robert A. Winston, published reprint 1939 by Holiday House, Inc.

Closing With the Enemy – How GI's Fought the War in Europe, 1944-1945, by Michael D. Doubter, 1944, by University Press of Kansas.

Fighting Squadrons, A Sequel to Dive Bomber by Robert A. Winston, published 1946 by Holiday House, Inc.

The Gathering Storm by Winston Churchill, published 1948 by Houghton Mifflin Co.

The Rise and Fall of The Third Reich – A History of Nazi Germany by William L. Shirer, copyright 1959, 1960 published by Fawcett Publications

Encyclopedia of Second World War, copyright 1989 published by Castle Books

Hocus Pocu*s* by Kurt Vonnegut, published 1990 by G. P. Putnam's Sons

The Bedford Boys, One American Town's Ultimate D-D Sacrifice by Alex Kershaw, published 2003 by Da Capo Press

Fly Boys – A True Story of Courage by James Bradley, published 2003 by Little Brown & Co.

The World War II Desk Reference With The Eisenhower Center for American Studies, Copyright 2004, Director Douglas Brinkley, Editor Michael E. Haskew, Harper Collins Publishers

The First Men In – U.S. Paratroopers and the Fight To Save D-Day by Ed Ruggero, copyright 2006 by Harper Colliers Publishers

My First and Only Paid Vacation 1942 – 1945 by Joseph L. Frank, copyright 2007, published by Trafford Publishers

Oceans of Love – A Collection of World War I Letters by B. J. Bryan, 2007, published by Trafford Publishers

The Ship That Never Was – A Story of U.S. Armed Guard and the Merchant Ships of World War II by B. J.

Bryan, published by Xlibris LLC, 2011

Escape With a Silent Roar – A Trilogy of Three World War Pilots by B. J. Bryan, 2013, published by Xlibris LLC

These are the men and women who accompanied Hank on the Honor Flight:

Henry G. Smith
Melvin Olsen
Edward Hook
Robert & Geneva Russell
Helen & Milan Popp
Richard Land
Howard Schonberger
Robert Upton

Accompanied by the ones responsible for this Honor Flight:

Barb Schwartz – 425 747 7057

Max Bettman – 206 384 4382
Cell phone No. 206 753 8139LC.

Appendices

APPENDIX 1

ANOTHER B-17 FLIGHT;
THIS TIME ABOARD THE
"SENTIMENTAL JOURNEY"

APPENDIX 2

BACK IN A B-17

APPENDIX 3

HONOR FLIGHT CERTIFICATE
OF RECOGNITION

APPENDIX 4

MAY 8: V-E DAY AT THE
WORLD WAR II MEMORIAL

APPENDIX 5

FREEDOM FIGHTERS HONOR FLIGHT

APPENDIX 6

WORLD WAR II VETERANS
INVOLVED IN THE NORMANY INVASION

"THE GREAT CRUSADE"

APPPENDIX 7

THE WINGS OF FREEDOM TOUR
CERTIFICATE FOR FLIGHT EXPERIENCE

www.ingramcontent.com/pod-product-compliance
Lightning Source LLC
Chambersburg PA
CBHW060950040426
42445CB00011B/1081